Swimming in the Ocean of Consciousness

Book 1

Elsio Eybrecht

Balboa Press books may be ordered through booksellers or by contacting:

Balboa Press
A Division of Hay House
1663 Liberty Drive
Bloomington, IN 47403
www.balboapress.com
1 (877) 407-4847

ISBN: 978-1-9822-3427-0 (sc)
ISBN: 978-1-9822-3428-7 (e)

Library of Congress Control Number: 2019913537

Print information available on the last page.

Balboa Press rev. date: 06/03/2020

BALBOA.PRESS
A DIVISION OF HAY HOUSE

ACKNOWLEDGEMENTS

<u>My Calling:</u>

The journey into Self, is one that truly is a calling onto.

From the depths of your soul, you will hear a voice that will resonate only with you, at a frequency that only you can comprehend with the heart. This is you, skimming a stone across the Ocean of Consciousness, contemplating your existence and discovering Self! This deep feeling of knowing your own truth, knowing the way that is for all, is the path of least resistance for all who seek.

This is the Ocean of Consciousness and the Tides of Life! It is your sense of Self from the physical into the mental and emotional. You must then seek beyond the horizon to discover the Source, the spiritual, which is beyond comprehension. From the emotional heart into the depths of Source or soul, into the depths of spirit or consciousness, this path of least resistance leads to the discovery of Self.

My calling has always been one of a spiritual nature ever since I was a child. I knew there was a purpose to this life for me, a purpose that eventually led me on a 25 year journey into the wilderness and to the discovery of Self and Source. This is where my interest into Self, began as a child, in my teen years and into adulthood. It was an innate need to be whole and complete, this need for answers or for truth. A truth that no one else seemed to have around me nor amidst this vast world, that I woke to find myself.

<u>The Road of many Miles, discovering Mentors and Friends along Life's Journey:</u>

Over the years, I have made many friends. I have had many mentors that saw something in me, that in those first moments I did not see in myself. Perhaps they saw something that was undeveloped and decided to assist me with the discovery of Self by being a mentor to guide me or a friend who wanted only the best for me.

I would like to acknowledge my mentors and friends alike with this publication of my first book. Without a support team of people in your life that can be voices of reason, encouragement and support, I would have had to face my own monsters of the mind and venture into this world of uncertainty with lesser courage and faith.

All the Girls, I've ever Loved:

This is where I first have to thank my grandmother for being my first spiritual teacher and guru for she was an amazing woman. She helped to shape and form the brave heart that I am today as I face this world of uncertainty. She instilled in me the courage that only faith can bring to a being that is neither here nor there but rather, anchored in light and resonating as a lighthouse of hope to all. I am also grateful for my mother and father for this life that I have been given. I am especially thankful to my mother for always being there when I was a child and for helping me to learn life's most important lesson to always believe in Self. I was blessed with a wonderful childhood, and it is those life lessons and memories that I carry with me into tomorrow for they are everlasting.

Life is a journey that we must live and experience for ourselves. Every so often, we come across people who we just vibe with and we feel it necessary to share with them our life, our bodies and our love in an intimate way. For me I have been blessed to have loved and to have been loved by many women over the years. Though they did not all last in romance, I always tried to be a friend to the end. I have been able to transition from each relationship with a life lesson with gratitude for their love for life and for me. Because of this, I want to say a special thanks to all of them. There have been times when I was loved while at my lowest in life, and it was that kind of unconditional love, blended with passion, that has nurtured me to complete my journey into Self. They have helped enable me to return as a whole and complete being into this world, to share with you my journey, my journey into Self or Source; "Swimming in the Ocean of Consciousness" and "The Art of Self-Transformation".

The Lady of the Lake:

The stream of consciousness, the Source that is all, is a stream of life energy that flows through life as tides, waves, streams and rivers that flow on two paths: One leads to the oceans and the other leads to our lakes. The lake is known as the "Body of Life" or the "Lady of the Lake." It is from this place within the Garden of Eden, within the inner chambers, that life came forth and man was created. It is through this gate that we must transcend in order to gain access to the light of Self.

The Art of Self-Transformation:

The Art of Self–Transformation, is the art of knowing self and awakening each day and living life in a moment of joy, love, light, hope, peace, radiance, healing, restoration, health and vigor. We all want change, but it has been my experience that very few want to stand in discipline to achieve their own healing. They won't show up and put in the work to know. It is only through knowing that we can gain a perspective by which to believe in anything. The journey begins within us. This journey is a journey of a single mile lived in a single moment. This is the story of life. This is our life story lived in a dream, a dream about love found, experienced, and then lost all in a single moment. This cruelty is also the sweetness of life as it is the making of love experienced in a single moment, this is the orgasmic bliss of life! We have to know that our purpose is movement or flow. We were created to flow through this life, just as water flows through the Earth. Just as the water flows and moves the Earth, it warms the Earth through fire water from the core. These two elements are essential to our lives just as love and lust are. They are essential to our transformation and the discovery of Self by Self through Self-cultivation, the process of the transformation of Self. Fire is for purification and water is for cleansing. Together they bring forth the natural healing from the Source of all. The air that we breathe, also gives us life but it is not the Source of our life.

These are all tides and waves within the ocean of consciousness, within the minds of man.

This book is the first in my series entitled "Swimming in the Ocean of Consciousness."

It is my story behind the visual and an introduction to my life experiences. It is the path that led me to my method and approach to transformational life coaching and the work that I do with my clients at annual transformational healing retreats.

I welcome and thank you for your support in purchasing my book, audio book or one of my video coaching series courses. Please visit my website and subscribe to my podcast to learn more about Swimming in the "Ocean of Consciousness" with Coach Elsio Eybrecht.

Elsio A.F. Eybrecht
September, 2019

Energy Body Activation
Conscious Mind-Body Meditation & Movement-

In Energy Body Activation, Coach Elsio Eybrecht will lead readers through his process of achieving Self-love and connection with his innate spiritual guidance. His journey will inspire readers to do the same. He guides them through the process of achievement, incorporating traditional health and fitness with holistic life coaching. He fuses the two to create Energy Body Activation.

There are three disciplines involved in this robust life-changing process:

- Stillness in Motion
- Poetry in Motion
- Passion in Motion

Elsio will guide the reader through this process, offering meditations, practical and actionable physical practices, affirmations and inspirations from his own experience and life story. The reader will come away from this experience with a newfound union of the physical body and the higher Self, allowing the possibility of unprecedented achievements.

Elsio Eybrecht is arguably one of the most innovative thought masters focused on the area of mind-body-spirit connection for the attainment of healing and alignment. An understanding mentor that has experienced significant challenges of his own shares his knowledge on how to overcome adversity, in the areas of physical, mental, and emotional wellbeing.

I came to know Elsio several years ago from traveling in similar circles of professional development seminars and online groups. We eventually solidified our friendship and business relationship online close to the same time he was experiencing a period of significant upheaval. I followed his trek from California to the East Coast and back to the West Coast, eventually settling in Seattle. It was during this time that I witnessed a transformation in Elsio. There were days he would talk about the darkness, the stillness and letting go. As his journey progressed, he spoke more frequently of finding light in the stillness, of finding enlightenment.

Nearly a century ago, Napoleon Hill said, "Every adversity, every failure, every heartbreak, carries with it the seed of an equal or greater benefit." Elsio was able to take those seeds of disappointment and strife and grow a life-changing business alongside many personal successes.

By discovering how to tune into his higher Self, Elsio has found his purpose as a life coach. He is a professional that can place himself into the mindset of others. He understands the challenges others face, and he can help them "get unstuck." He has an undying reputation as a transformational speaker, author, and life coach.

In this text, Elsio shares his journey to finding enlightenment and infinite intelligence. At the age of sixteen, he developed a love for teaching tennis. Then unexpectedly, he faced the probability that he may never play tennis again, or even run. The young Elsio began focusing on what his life options were and found hope in the stillness of the mind. He spent much time reading and meditating. Eventually, he found an inner peace upon which to build a firm foundation. He was able to elevate not just his mind, but his physical body and spirit as well.

Since those days, Elsio has continued to overcome challenges, and even when some days were bleak, he persisted. In 2015, he experienced the failure of business investments, along with a divorce and the loss of his beloved grandmother. Instead of rolling in self-pity, he picked himself up, and, along with his best canine friend, Buster, and made a fresh start. Eventually, Elsio would find himself in Seattle, where he now calls home. He runs his coaching and wellness businesses here also.

In life, there are always people who can talk a good talk but haven't walked that same talk. Elsio, teaches from experience and is genuinely one of the few authentic life coaches I have had the pleasure to know. His story is incredibly powerful as is his ability to be empathetic.

One thing Elsio has said repeatedly that resonated with me was, "A person has to be willing to show up each day. Tomorrow is there for the taking, but we have to rise to the challenge, and take it."

Elsio Eybrecht takes you on a journey into what he calls the Sea of Consciousness, as a starting point for finding enlightenment and the higher Self. He will explain what body-energy is and how to start healing and conquering from the inside mind out.

Whether you are an athlete looking to improve your game, or a person who has experienced significant health challenges, consider this text as a starting point to reach a singular destination. Know that this book was written by a person who has experience working through obstacles, has rebounded, and desires to make the world a better place. It is a tool for helping others attain a better life, good health, and positive wellbeing.

—Lanna Monday Emmett

Lanna Monday Emmett is an assistant professor of Visual Communications at Tusculum University who owns an independent digital media communication business. She holds multiple degrees from East Tennessee State University and a graduate degree from Quinnipiac University.

As one looks back on their life, one begins to realize how the journey to the present was affected to a large extent by certain people that intersected your path. Elsio is one of those people who showed up in my life one day with a clear passion to accomplish something bold in his home country, especially for a young man at that time. With a gleam in his eye and a conviction in his vision for developing a tennis center in St. Maarten, it was clear Elsio was on a mission. Little did he know perhaps that his mission was bigger than even he may had realized.

Over 18 years have passed since that first day in my office, during which we exchanged countless conversations about his vision for business, but more importantly about our beliefs that guide us, that drive us, that opens our soul to a larger reality that is so often so difficult to understand sometimes, let alone articulate.

He left his country and those that were close to him for it seemed he couldn't accomplish what he was destined to do there. Having many conversations during the tumult that led to his departure, his connections to the U.S. led him to Michigan. What could be more out of one's comfort zone than leaving the Caribbean to end up living in Michigan during the winter? It was there that I leaned of the deeper journey that Elsio was on.

As an architect, I dream of the "uncreated" which eventually manifests into physical reality, an intervention or environment that I hope would bring what the late architect Will Alsop called "joy and delight". Referring to what he believed we in the profession were involved in as opposed to all other professions involved in "doom and gloom". The first century B.C. Roman architect Marcus Vitruvius described that architecture should be founded on the principles of "commodity, firmness, and delight" where delight in fact referred to venustas, or "beauty". Leonardo DaVinci's illustration of the Vetruvian man connects me then back to Elsio. While the beauty and sensuality of the human form fascinated Elsio, it was his deeper connection with the spiritual self where he connected with me. Elsio was the contemporary Vetruvian Man not because of supreme proportions of nature and thus beauty.

Elsio was connecting the spiritual with the physical where beauty is connected to the inner-self and strength through the connection with the spiritual. While my own spiritual journey was rocking my world, Elsio's journey was something else. He had already been through heart-ache and emotional distress. He was learning that there was more to his personal journey, more that he had to discover, more that he was to experience.

During his years on the West Coast, there were more set-backs. As he was acclimating to a new environment and discovering a new partner, he was also refining his methodology for training. His methodology was rooted in connecting mind-body-spirit. I believe he was also learning more about the himself and what was possible as continued preparation for what was to come.

While developing his new business venture, the possibilities seemed bigger than even he could have hoped for. Elsio thinks big. I admire him for that.

I wanted him to succeed in such a big way. Alas, as life is, obstacles always seem to be lurking around the corner, somehow to materialize and dampen the positive spirit. He was moving towards the cusp of something new and bold, yet it appeared that his time was not to be yet. Broken partnerships, tremendous heart ache, and what seemed to be the disintegration of his dreams were to challenge his resolve.

Several years later, he has emerged on the Pacific Northwest to discover that vision doesn't die. There are successes and there are set backs and the rhythm of life is a constant to and fro. It is the bold that experiences this rhythm at another level, amplified by the degree of boldness one lives life. I am hearing in him the absorption of these experiences through a new filter, a new mechanism for enlightenment. Through the lens of hindsight, the maturation of his methodology for training was converging with his methodology for life. In competition sport such as tennis, you win or you lose. One has to choose to persevere through loss in order to win. To Elsio, each set-back is the dusk before a new dawn. Now dusk is the promise of dawn and there is a supreme beauty in both.

I don't think I would call Elsio an eternal optimist. He has become a new realist with a dream that never dies. He is someone no different than you or I who has the spirit to succeed and the resolve to rise. Through stillness, poetry and passion, Elsio modulates his rhythms of life. It is his own "firmness, commodity and delight". His focus has become emboldened. To me, the Vetruvian Man which I connected with over eighteen years ago has risen from Leonardo DaVinci's page and is not only an inspiration in today's world of confusion, pain, and heart-ache, but evidence that whatever one goes through, there can be a new dawn for self-fulfillment and transformation.

James (Jim) Renne, A.I.A

It is no secret that healing does not happen if you are singularly focused. If you choose to go the traditional medical route, you may see some improvement but not complete healing. Likewise, if you focus solely on holistic methods, you may make strides, but a full sense of wellness may still elude you. For this reason, the integration of movement into any healing routine is vital to make leaps and bounds toward healing and achieving personal and spiritual goals.

In a spiritual sense, we may find ourselves lost and unable to connect to Spirit because of the rampant mind, body, and soul discord. The constant static of our day-to-day lives with the business that plagues our society. We are on the go, never stopping to open our minds to the vast expanse that exists beyond what we know.

In the physical body, we suffer from more injuries than ever before—orthopedic and beyond. Also, many of us struggle to maintain a balanced, healthy, and happy life due to some injury or illness. I am living proof that you can survive and ultimately recover from the worst physical trauma. Even if doctors give up on your recovery, Source has other plans.

The following is my journey leading to the story of Coach Elsio Eybrecht. It describes how I have survived spinal surgery and lived not just to walk again but to thrive in the game of tennis, stay healthy, and become a fitness coach.

In the depths of my despair, I never imagined that my painful surgery would eventually lead to better days and opportunities. From the struggle, I found myself completing the Chek Institute Holistic Life Coach Program and launched my own business as a transformational author, speaker, and life coach.

THE HAWK THAT LEARNED TO SOAR

Before I begin to explain just what this "Energy-Body activation" is, I would like to explain just how it came to be. I was in the process of recovering from major spinal surgery, after which I was advised by my doctor to give up tennis. He also suggested I avoid any other physically challenging activities that could further damage my spine or cause my existing injury to flare up again.

You must understand that I did not take this advice lightly. I carefully analyzed and considered what the doctor was telling me. I lay there in my hospital bed, reflected on my life, and looked closely at where I was at that moment of my life. I looked at my legs just lying there; I was hardly able to move them. They were so weak that I could not stand or walk on my own. I was amazed at how small they had become due to the decline in my muscle tissue thanks to inactivity.

It's surprising how many thoughts can run through one's mind when one is in such a position or in any situation that leaves one feeling so helpless and hopeless! I was scared. I won't lie! I cried for many nights and had trouble sleeping. However, after those tears dried, I had a decision to make. I kept asking myself, "What would I do with the rest of my life? How do I find the strength and the courage to walk away from a lifelong dream? How do I bury my goals and move on?" For many sleepless nights, I ruminated on these questions.

In this time, I became heavily reliant upon myself, and I began to understand I was a very spiritual being. Even before the accident that caused my spinal injury, I was on a personal spiritual quest—one of spiritual evolution. I wanted to know the answers to life's three basic questions: who am I, from where do I come, and to where do I go?

Before my accident, I was a religious person, but I soon found religion itself did not have the answers to the questions that I was asking. I soon began my quest for spiritual truth—spiritual truth about my being, my life, the world in which I existed, and the universe in which that world existed.

I had so much free time on my hands while just lying in my hospital bed for three months after my surgery. I had to be strong enough to stand on my own. I was ready to learn how to walk again. Yes. I had to learn how to walk all over again.

I used this time to read as much as I could from the various wisdom texts that I had purchased before going to the hospital. As I would wait for the nurse to come and give me my regular fix of morphine every three hours to ease my intense pain, I would stay up late at night reading. I would lie in bed meditating, on the things that I was learning all the while discovering myself. I was also gaining insight into the bigger picture of the world at large.

When I had regained enough strength to stand on my own, it was time to leave the hospital and go home. My doctor then suggested that I visit with a physical therapist to aid in the rehabilitation of my muscles so that I could walk and move around regularly and independently. After a few months of this, I realized the therapists had helped me as much as they could. The rest would be up to me.

Most of what they were doing with me, I already knew how to do on my own. I used to teach the same basic movements to my clients during our tennis and fitness classes. So I decided to seek assistance from deep within myself, to search the depths of my subconscious mind. I came to realize that if a man honestly had a soul and if this soul of man was somehow connected to or linked to the supreme soul of all—the god of all gods—then I would learn to discipline my mind and learn how to channel my mental energy within. I would find a way to make a connection to this essence of life and to see if I could find the answers to my questions about life. I desired to have the wisdom and knowledge to heal my physical body.

Enlightenment is not an overnight thing. It is not just something or someplace that one stumbles upon simply because one desires it. Instead, it is a journey—a life-changing journey—on which we must all embark. I learned that enlightenment was not the end but just the beginning. It is the beginning of life as it should be lived!

I also became aware of the essence of life, including the vital energy that flows through us unseen. This energy allows us all to be who we are, what we are when we are, and what we desire to be.

With this wisdom, I combined what I learned in my readings. I then added to that my experience from tennis, fitness, and living a healthy lifestyle. I was able to revive my body from a state of living dead.

I came to realize that anyone who has the ability to move all parts of the freely, then that person should be grateful. All people should use this opportunity to live an active and healthy lifestyle, for movement is king, and proper breathing is a queen. Together, they are the key to life.

Some may say for one to know of the Self and to attain enlightenment, a guide is necessary—a so-called spiritual leader or guru. However, it is possible for someone to come to know of one's Self without the guidance of such a person. It just takes time and commitment.

THE BIG WHY

One only needs to honestly and sincerely seek, and one shall find! For it is said, "No sooner is one ready to see, then one will see. And no sooner is one ready to hear, then one will hear." An individual only needs to be ready to receive, and the cosmic forces of nature will provide one with what one needs to survive. The forces have done this from the beginning of time and space, and they will continue to do this indefinitely. Unfortunately, we live in a time and space in which many of us are deaf, dumb, and blind to the truth about ourselves. We are blind to the truth about life, about this world, and our place in it.

It does not mean that having a spiritual guru is necessarily the best path to enlightenment. Many roads travel to the same final destination. One must remember that there is just one singular destination. From the beginning of time, before there were any wisdom texts written or recorded by man, there was the truth! While this truth was eventually discovered and shared by mankind, one may wonder, "From whom or where did it originate?"

In today's modern times, there are many spiritual leaders spread all over the world professing to have the keys to life. It may even seem at times that they are on every block of every city, all promising and promoting enlightenment under their guidance. It almost gives the appearance of a franchise on the rise, a new age phenomenon of sorts, similar to Starbucks coffee shops! Why is this happening, and why now?

As mankind evolves, it simply means that there is a divine essence within us all that more and more individuals are becoming attuned to. This inner voice—this in-born concept of life, the will to live, and this inner guide to the kingdom of God—is in us all. It's in every living creature created by His word upon the face of the earth. At any one single moment in a person's life, one can truly be ready to receive divine guidance and can receive it. Once our heart has found balance upon the scale of truth, weighed against the feather of truth, it has been said, " You may look me in the eye and lie, but what shall you do when it is your heart that is being weighed in against the feather? How will you lie on that day?"

This enlightenment is for all to discover in this lifetime. The world needs peace, love, and unity amongst her children. It should be the work of a spiritual leader—to bring the truth to the people, not to keep it hidden as some ancient secret when times have evolved and modernized.

We were not living five or ten thousand years ago, we are living right now, in the present moment, in a trying and turbulent time and space. There is a great need for spiritual evolution among the world's children to sit back and enjoy being praised as master and lord.

I say, "This is the way is for ALL."

I had to be very careful not to force my body beyond the point that it was ready and willing to go. The body is like bamboo, though it is very flexible, if forced and pushed beyond a certain point, it will break.

Everything has a breaking point!

My first lesson: Listen to your body.

You are not the body, and the body is not you! With this in mind, and with my in-born spiritual guidance, I began to slowly stretch and move my physical body, gaining the necessary flexibility and mobility to move increasingly forward on my road to recovery.

I must admit that the ocean helped a lot. I spent much time in the sea, just floating in the water and gently swimming, remaining cautious not to force my body. However, still, this period of my life was not without failure and frustration. So, I learned how to see the good in everything. I learned how to seize every moment, good or bad.

My second lesson: Be patient and trust yourself.

The definition of frequency is the rate at which something occurs over a specific time. In this case, I am referring to the frequency and energy levels. We all exist in time and space, and everything that exists in time and space vibrates with its unique frequency. In the case of humans, some may exhibit high rates, while others may vibrate at a lower frequency. Every individual possesses his or her unique energy, created from the culmination of mind, body, and soul. Therefore every individual vibrates on a unique frequency. The only limitations are that every person is:

- Bound by the laws of gravity
- Bound by the forces of nature

I had to learn to be myself before I could begin to believe in myself. I had to allow my mind and subconscious to trust in what I could not see, hear, or touch but could feel, deep down in my being. I had to surrender to my soul. I had to allow it to be the captain of my vessel as I journeyed across the ocean of consciousness. I had to be the product of what I was created to be. I had to learn to be without thought, doubt or fear. I had to learn to be, without any apology.

It was at this time that I slowly began to learn just how to feel myself¬—how to know myself—how to be, without being. I learned to exist from a tranquil place within myself, a place void of all thoughts and all emotions. It was here that I became conscious of my soul and of what is known as infinite power. I became aware of my life force energy—the light of my life, the soul of my soul. The Chinese call this force Qi or Chi. The Hindus call this force Kundalini. Early Egyptians knew it as Arat-Sekhem or the Serpent Power of Life.

This life force energy lies dormant within us all, waiting to awaken.

It was through this newfound wisdom and knowledge of myself—of my higher Self—I understood and gained through my spirit through my in-born guide. I channeled life force energy. I channeled the energy of the spine base to the skull crown. This movement is what is known as the coiling and uncoiling of the Serpent of Life.

Once this life force energy began to flow through my body, I began to feel it. I could feel the effect of its fire as it set my soul ablaze and burned out all impurities from within my being. I call it, "The fire in the back."

My third lesson: Let go and surrender to what is more significant than what you are.

It was at this time that this life force began to create a sort of clarity in my conscious mind. I compare it to having a window in your house, and over time (from one's birth to the moment of enlightenment) this window becomes dirty with the dust of life (the illusions of life.) One day you suddenly realize that it is time to clean this window. You spray Windex on it and wipe it clean with a cloth. From this moment on, the view from the window has changed. Suddenly you can see more. You believe you can see more. You see more of what was always there. You begin to appreciate and understand all of the beauty of life that you see from this window. You now understand the bigger picture. You now know the part you play in this beautiful world that you see through your window.

This life force energy strengthened my body from the inside out. It was as if suddenly I realized that it was not the movement of my body, but that the action was I. I understood that this movement came from a place deep within me—from a place of stillness.

At that moment, I let go.

I let go. I never held on again. I was re-born. That was the moment that I arose from the dead, and I learned to live once more. I learned how to live as a man. I learned all of this through seeking within my being, and not outside. I learned all of this by trusting my soul and not putting my trust in another man.

Now, today, I am, that I am, I am.

I am what I am. I am where I am, from the place where I am from, and headed to the place from where I've come.

This is the journey of my soul. This is the journey of my life. It is my life's purpose. I learned this through being brave and courageous enough to trust and to believe in that which I could not see—to hear what I could not hear, but feel in my mind and my heart.

I learned to live again through blind faith.

With a new body, a fresh mind and, a freed soul, I began to train again. I combined the wisdom and knowledge gained through my studies of the wisdom text of old, the disciplines of yoga (divine union of the higher & lower Self,) and my regular tennis training and fitness skills. I allowed my purified mind and soul to be my guide along the way.

I found myself practicing precise movements of the body. However, I noticed I was performing these movements not with my body, but instead with my unconscious mind—not with my intellect mind of reasoning, but with my causal mind. I found these new movements were used in the training and development of tennis skills and cardio fitness routines. In fact I found myself using the actions in my day-to-day life—in everything from walking to talking, from sitting to standing and bending over to squatting down. The motor skills required to function in my daily life were now being performed as with certain poetry and grace. That's what I began to call this, "*Poetry in motion.*"

My movements and thoughts stemmed from within my mind—a place of stillness, a place of peace, or hetep. (Hetep is an Egyptian word that means to be at peace.) I called this, "*Stillness in motion.*"

Feeling the flow of my life force energy as it moved through my body, I came to understand that this pure Source of life-giving power was God's passion for life. It was his creative mind; it was his desire to be—therefore, it was his passion, so I called this, "*Passion in motion.*"

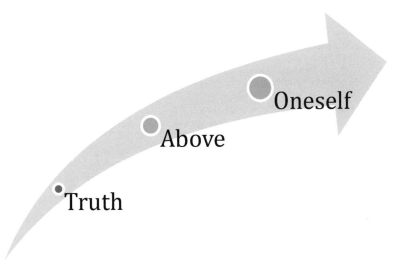

The Tao of Tennis Method was born from the life-changing experience I lived through on my journey to Self-discovery. These three phrases I use, to sum up, what I've learned, helped me to gain a better understanding of my life, body, mind, and soul. This method also helped me to return to my craft or art, which was my profession, the sport of tennis.

It came to be that through my newly acquired wisdom and knowledge of Self and art, The Tao of Tennis was born.

In this book, Energy Body Activation: Conscious Mind-Body Meditation & Movement for Beginners, I will introduce you to this system of Energy-Body Activation. It consists of three disciplines:

1. Stillness in Motion

2. Poetry in Motion

3. Passion in Motion

I am sharing with you the wisdom and knowledge I have gained throughout my journey across the sands of time—the journey that has brought me to where I am today!

I do not believe that anyone being or race has the right to claim any superior wisdom or knowledge about life or the soul of man. Neither does any individual or race have the right to hold in secrecy the keys to spiritual evolution. Wisdom and knowledge were given to humankind to evolve into a higher Self, apart from living like an animal. to stand and walk upright as a 'God-Man.' One who reaches this level should find it within the inner Self to share that knowledge with the rest of humanity.

To receive this wisdom and knowledge and not to share it with one's brothers and sisters is a direct violation of the unwritten laws of life. To quote an old piece of wisdom, "To give is to give freely. To receive is having given that which was never yours to hold onto." So it is with this in mind that I share my wisdom with the hopes that you, the reader, will find somewhere in this book, the inspiration, and motivation to seek the wisdom for yourself. My goal is to present to you a different option, a different way to become aware of your higher Self in this single lifetime.

Living from the Energy-Body while mastering the art of conscious mind-body meditations and movements, will facilitate a new view on life. It will present a different way of living life from joy and happiness. Know that the stream from the Source is constant. The Ocean of Consciousness is vast.

HOTEP: SUPREME PEACE BE WITH YOU

I have been grateful to have learned from Paul Chek, who shares his unique approach to preventing orthopedic injury. He helps his clients improve performance through nutrition and optimal motor engram programming.

His concept, fused with my Stillness in Motion - Poetry in Motion - Passion in Motion Philosophy in mind, I have built a series of energy body activation movements, to catalyze spiritual and physical healing.

Begin this sequence slowly, taking five minutes to repeat each. Start incorporating it into your routine once a week, then three times, and, finally, flow through it each day.

Elsio's Swimming in the Ocean of Consciousness Affirmation

Life is a long road to the gates of heaven. Sometimes in life, I will take that bus ride alone, and other times, I will find someone willing to take that bus ride with me.

The scenery always changes. I have to treasure each moment and move forward and onward on the journey of life. I will not be left behind, waiting by the bus stop for the right moment and the right bus. I will live my life with faith and purpose-driven by my destiny!

I will live from my heart and let the joy and happiness that is within me be my message to the world and let the loving-kindness that is my connection to my Source be a guiding light through the darkest of night.

Hetep - Supreme peace be with you!

—*Coach Elsio Eybrecht*
Affirmation #1

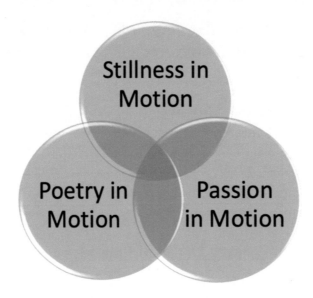

Stillness in Motion

Stillness in Motion is a focused meditation into the Ocean of Consciousness paired with slow energy body-work meant to ignite the life energy fire from within.

Guided Meditation and Focalized Point of Attraction:

Skimming a Stone Out to Sea

One day I witnessed a man running. It seemed as though he had been running for a very long time. As he approached the seashore, he slowed down as if the smell of the ocean breeze drew him. He jogged over to the water's edge. He stood there as if lost in a moment—as if he was reflecting—meditating on his life.

He then looked down and picked up a stone. He looked deeply at the rock as if he recognized it. He seemed to touch it with affection. Then, I watched him turn, and as he gazed out to sea, he skimmed the stone out over the water's edge. As the stone approached the water, it skimmed on the rough seas surface. It seemed to pick up momentum as it hit each wave. Eventually, it sunk deep into the ocean and was out of sight. At that moment, the man seemed to return to his "Self" and resumed running down the beach.

THEMES TO RECOGNIZE

- The smell of the ocean is the awakening of one's Self.
- The stone in hand is to look deeply at thy Self with loving-kindness.
- The skimming of the stone over rough seas is the trials & tribulations of everyday life.
- The stone gaining momentum against all the odds of the rough seas is the persistence of Spirit allowing Self to connect to the Source within.
- The skimming out over the ocean is the Self within swimming in the Ocean of Consciousness.
- The stone sinking into the ocean is the Self as it surrenders to Source and becomes one.
- The man, returning to his Self, is the life within always coming full circle back to Self.

I know all of this because I was that man running down to the water's edge. It was my in my own experience that I that looked down and picked up that stone. It was me that skimmed it out to sea and reaped the benefit of understanding the bigger picture.

THE FIVE STATES OF CONSCIOUSNESS WITHIN THE OCEAN OF CONSCIOUSNESS

1. The Ego-Conscious State of Being

2. The Self-Awareness or Self-Conscious State of Being

3. The Subconscious State of Being

4. The Unconscious State of Being

5. The Nothingness of the Source-Conscious State of Being

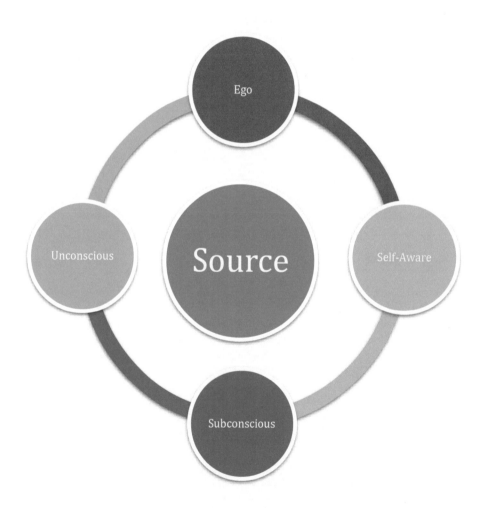

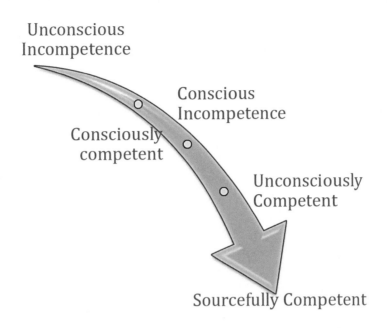

The Four Stages of Learning in Life and How to Make the Most of Them

Even the most educated and distinguished person in today's busy society has within them the ability to touch and connect with their higher Self, inner being and, from that place, to discover how to become a better human being through the art of Self-cultivation.

If a person becomes conscious weaknesses and works on them from a place of peace with honesty and healing light, there is no limit to the potential of this life. When learning how to live and discovering how to be one's Self, he or she will pass through four stages of learning. These four stages are not specific to one aspect of life or focus. These stages are part of the physiological makeup of humans.

The mental energy, our life energy, and our spiritual energies, all beautifully blend to give a sense of life experience or experiencing life in a given moment of time and space.

Knowing which stage one is in at the moment, and how to make the best of it, will shorten the learning time/curve and free one from limitations.

The First Stage: Unconscious Incompetence

When a person is unconsciously incompetent, he or she does not even know that he or she is not skilled.

Ignorance is bliss, as has been said. In this stage, there's nothing a person can do directly since you he or she does not even know that he or she is missing something.

However, while one may not be precisely aware of what is explicitly missing, it is probable that something is missing.

So what works best in this stage is:

- Accumulating much knowledge about goals.
- Observing how others who have reached similar goals behave.

These actions will help to become more aware of the steps needed to reach any goals.

The Second Stage: Conscious Incompetence

Once aware of what's missing in life's plan, one becomes conscious of it.

The problem is known, but the fix is not.

The reason for that is, of course, lack of practice and repetition. The more complex the task and the bigger the goal, the longer it will take to reach it.

The best way to shorten this stage is to:

- Focus on work.
- Be patient.

While one may intellectually know what needs to happen, the body cannot learn as quickly. It needs more repetition to be able to learn a new movement. Patience and waiting for the body to catch up with the mind is the best method.

Another key to becoming competent (skilled) is to focus on a single task. Don't try to work on too many things at once. For example, in tennis, if a person is working on a forehand technique, then he or she should focus only on this technique and not try to improve footwork, tactics, and speed at the same time.

The focus becomes split between four different tasks. Therefore none will be mastered. Remember, the body needs many repetitions to make a lasting change.

The Third Stage: Conscious Competence

If a person continues working on a skill, eventually he or she will "get it." He or she will achieve that "Ah-ha!" moment and be able to make the right move for the first time. The individual will also probably feel a new sensation. It is the signal that this is the movement the person needed.

That means that one has just become consciously competent.

In this stage, one can perform the movement correctly, must keep reminding the Self (being conscious) of what needs to happen. Examples in the game of tennis include keeping your grip loose, lifting your racquet head, and extending through the ball.

As soon as one forgets or starts focusing on something else (become unconscious again), he or she will go back to the old technique (or skill).

The key to shortening this stage is the same as in the second stage:

- Focus only on one thing at a time.
- Repeat the process to store the new information in the subconscious.

If learning more aspects of a movement, remain focused on and dedicated to the basics. Practice for five minutes and focus only on the basics. The rest will not perfect, but it is not crucial in this stage. The goal is to store information at the subconscious level with "continuous, uninterrupted" repetition. Store the feeling of the basics for five minutes (focus on it.) Then switch to the next task, perhaps take it one step further.

Keep switching from task to task for many sessions. Eventually, try to link them. Likely, they will already have become part of the unconscious and work together well without the conscious effort to connect them.

The Fourth Stage: Unconscious Competence

The more a new skill is rehearsed and practiced, the greater likelihood it will become an automatic response. The person will become unconsciously competent, which means that he or she will be able to perform a new skill (a new stroke or improved technique) without thinking about it. It will free the mind for other tasks. The individual will be able to work on other weaknesses while building toward a goal. A person can be able to focus on tactics and various ways of outplaying an opponent, or if the goal is singular, pushing harder or going faster. The technique will be completely unconscious and will become a tool for solving a tactical problem.

There's nothing more needed in this stage regarding the newly acquired skill. One can return to the first stage and explore what else is missing and can be improved. Once conscious of these four stages of learning, an individual can identify which he or she is, as it sets the stage to accelerate learning through the curve.

Life Is an Attitude

Life is a journey. One must ask one's Self if he or she is ready to discover the art of living, the art of elf-transformation, as one finds his or her inner guide, and the higher Self. There are no rules, no boundaries; one can never get it wrong. Wherever an individual stands, he or she will have a fresh new start now. One only needs to be consciously aware of which of the four stages of learning one is.

One's mental posture toward a situation or a problem is one of attraction. We live in an attraction based universe. A person must be conscious of the target of attention. It is how outcomes are attracted.

A person's feelings and one's emotions, about a problem or situation, is how one feels in the moment that he or she stands consciously competent. Emotions are a guide through this life and personal journey. Let joy be what one experiences in every moment. Suffering is not necessary to know. Release the fear and doubt in the heart and life and discover joy from within. Life is an attitude, and a person gets to choose how he or she feels in the here and now!

The angle or position of one's frame of mind /frame of reference or one's perspective on life is only a reflection of the alignment with the inner being. It is closely related to where a person finds themselves in each singular moment of the four stages of consciousness scale. It has to feel good, or it just is not for the person. The release is the cure for which humanity is searching. Life is a process. Allow the process to move through the mind, body, and soul. Resistance prevents aligning with the inner being. Remember that the way is for all. This is the concept of Tao:

- T-Truth
- A-Above
- O-One's Self
  or
- T-Truth
- A-Above
- O-Others

Be true to Self. Be true to the spirit. Be true to the gifts in life. Lead life by example. Be the person who is meant to be living in this life.

The art of allowing is the process of release. Let go of any resistance and go with the stream of life. Flow out to the depths of the ocean of consciousness. Contrast is necessary for change to manifest in life. Fear, not the seasons for they bring about the changes in life. Allow the emotional process to move emotions and feelings in the right direction.

Say to out loud daily, "I care about how I feel in my here and now. My feelings let me know how attuned I am to my Source, in my here and now. My Source is my inner light and my guiding light, my emotional guide on this journey of life. I am a lighthouse of hope for all of my family, friends, and humanity that they too may find their way amidst the vast ocean of consciousness."

Definition:

Attitude: A mental posture toward a problem or a situation; one's feelings or emotions toward a problem; the angle or perspective of one's frame of reference.

Your Definition:

_____

_____

List five ingredients that make up your attitude on life:

1 _____

2 _____

3 _____

4 _____

5 _____

Always remember, that when faced with a difficult situation in life, stop for a moment, take a deep breath and take a moment to reflect within to find balance with Self and Source. Create balance from within through a focalized point of attraction or consciousness. Regulate breathing and activate your energy-body!

ENERGY BODY ACTIVATION
CONSCIOUS MIND-BODY AFFIRMATION,
MEDITATION & MOVEMENT FOR BEGINNERS

Self-Transformation Affirmation:

Take a moment to read the following affirmation, and then, spend a few minutes reflecting on it before beginning exercises:

As I close my eyes, I can feel the life force that I am. I let go of all of the self-judgments of my being, and I give myself a warm and loving embrace. I now have permission to forgive myself and heal my heart. I will let the hurt and pain turn into a guiding light, and will turn that light out into the world and be a lighthouse of hope as I guide others out into the Ocean of Consciousness.

I am present to Self. I am aligned with my light and love. I will allow my energy body to activate with my life energy and my breath energy.

I have achieved Energy-Body activation.

Putting Teachings into Practice

Now that you have read and reflected on this affirmation, begin to slowly take action.

Stillness In Motion

Stillness in Motion is the ability to gain control of the conscious mind. It is through becoming Self-aware and making a conscious choice to separate from the ego-conscious state of being. First, find stillness.

Please find a comfortable seat. There is no specific posture or position necessary. Lay down on a yoga mat, sit up—anything that won't cause discomfort, as this will distract from making a deeper connection with Self, and discovering your inner guide. Always remember it is about Self-love and being kind to Self. It is a conscious action. From this place of stillness, you will focus on your breathing:

1. Lay down or sit comfortably.

2. Close your eyes and visualize Self.

3. Regulate breathing.

4. Allow the conscious mind to fuse with the body breathing. It will allow an open connection to the inner guide or your Energy-Body.

5. Release your breath. It is at this moment when you accept your connection to IG or higher Self, through this stillness.

The motion that connects to the stillness happens when one is comfortably breathing from a focalized point of attraction. To begin, slowly practice moving the body, but not from or with the ego conscious state of being.

Instead, allow your Energy-Body or higher Self to learn how to move the physical body. It is where the magic happens, where a tingly feeling will enable discovery of the Poetry in your Motion. Open your heart and let the Source stream flow through without the need for possession.

POETRY IN MOTION

First, concentrate on fluidity in the movement that is all at once activating, energizing, and meditative. The goal is mind, breath, and life energy fire alignment into smooth rhythmic, poetic energy body movement. Try to create a flow that feels fluid and natural, so the body encompasses learning, being, and doing. It may include strength training.

Strength suggestions:

- Push ups from a plank position
- Squats
- Six directional lunges
- Split jumping lunge
- Life energy ball balance work
- Slow Indian club
- Mace movement

31

PASSION IN MOTION

It is now time to take that fluidity and put it into action, performing fitness tasks that require full-body cooperation and alignment.

This practice involves running with a focus first on balance, posture, and movement of the body with the breathing from the focalized point of attraction. Begin by working toward completing one mile or one lap around the track. It is the basis from which to build the life fire-energy into one singular point of attraction. It aligns the mind, breath, and body as one single unit.

From the one-mile run, which is not about time but rather about connecting all of the above-mentioned independent skills, move to the next level. It is time to take the next step toward personal fitness and wellness goals and eventual transformation.

At the intermediate level, a total of 3 one-mile runs per week should be the baseline. Now the question is: Are you ready to accept the challenge of combining those three miles into one solid, but smooth, three-mile run per week?

To get there, start by focusing on the six directional lunges we discussed under the Poetry in Motion discipline section. It is how to begin strengthening the knees and quads to handle pounding the pavement for the entire length of the three-mile run.

It is where one joins the mind, body, and spirit through breath and a focalized point of attraction. It is where an individual will be able to begin to push the physical body to train for speed on the track and uphill sprints. One learns to tap into the Energy-Body when needed, to develop balance and strength or thrust, which will be useful in high-performance moments. With this foundation, the body will be able to provide a support system for breathing and focus. It will allow smooth flow and rhythm to complete an endurance run, such as a 10K or Half Marathon (13.1 Miles).

40

Born a Masterpiece
The Keeper of Time and Space, A Living Clock of Life!

There will be times of uncertainty, and there will be times of unrest, amidst this Season of turmoil know who you are! Fear not the words of those who fight against the Will of the Almighty but rather lend your ear to that whisper, Know that with a clear and definite Purpose along with a plan of action that is diligently focused upon from a conscious point of attraction and worked on daily with vigour and vitality will soon come to pass. For the Harvest is reaped not when the seeds are planted but in due season by His Grace and Mercy.!.

Some say it's Magic and some say it's Faith! But we are all born of the same Star Dust, we are all reflections of the Cosmic Ocean of Consciousness. Learn how to swim, and learn how to thread water for we are not born of this land, unless we are Man. For then, time is but a dream within a dream!

Men of this kind is our humanity through time. So it is only natural for us to dream of a world that is in alignment with the star lit heavens. This is our Holy Land or more so, our Land that is Whole and Complete, for so Above as Below! We are the missing link, We who have such Benevolent Hearts filled with Grace and Mercy equal to the Wrath of the Gods.

It is you...

You are the Mirror and the Reflection, you are this Masterpiece reflecting back across the ocean of consciousness. You are filled with Love and Light that must awaken from your illusive dream and tune your Thoughts, your Heart and your Intentions upon the Source and the Frequency Of the Holy Land, upon that place where we are all One, Known to those of Kind as Zion...

When you feel the shift in the Energy from your own mind or from someone else outside of your being. One who is trying to shame you into feeling bad about Self. This is when the Calibration of Self to Source is most necessary. This is when that Pause, that silent Note is played. They want for you to break down and become worried and filled with fear, so much so that you cannot rise and give Thanks and Praise for all that you are for that is the Golden Moment of Ignition, of Energy Body Activation when you Live your life with Purpose!

This is the Key to your Transformation, you simply must know who you are and that you are able and capable of shinning as bright as a Lighthouse, as Bright as the Star of the Night. You are the Living Sun, you are the Rainbow Light, Bright enough to guide all of those Men of Kind. Be a Source of Guidance and Inspiration to your Fellow Man! But you must always know and remember "Who You Are", "Know Thy Self" for Thou Art Born a Masterpiece, a Living Clock of Time and Space. A Heart of Consistency, that Guides your Way across the Vast Ocean upon your Journey of Life and Death...

A Mind as Vast as the Depths of the Ocean of Consciousness, this Pearl that is our Earth, this Shine in my Eye, this Joy and Laughter in my Heart, this Happiness is Love and this Love is the Light of my Soul. A Spirit that Roams as Free and Wild as the Winds of Time and the Stallion as He Rides, as He Rides the great Shimmering Wave upon the Sea Shores, touching the Minds, the Hearts and the Hands of Man, as He Rides across the reaches of Space and Time!

His Light forever a shining glimmer within the Eyes of Man. For there You were Born a master Piece, Created Whole and Complete even before your conception. You do not need to be told how great you are in order to feel good about who you are internally for you are Light and love.

Be not afraid nor ashamed to fall to your knees when you are weak and remember to give Praise with each Breath.... Give praise in Silence and give praise in Song. Always lift your head as your heart, to the Heavens and know that you are Born a Winner, You are Born a Masterpiece as you are the light of the Fathers Eye, His Radiance resides within your Heart....

Be Grateful for all that you are, be Grateful for the Journey and for those stones which were cast as those pebbles upon which you stumble for all that you can ever achieve and acquire is nothing without the Light that is You, the Grace that shines through all of the dark clouds!

Stand Firm on your own Merit, you are the Way, and you are the Light, you are the Hidden Key to an Ancient Lock!

Judge not your short comings, nor that of your fellow man. For now you see that this Life, is one of Trials and Tribulations made by the Minds and Hearts of Man. So it is, that only Man can free himself from this fog. You must always tune to your Source, for even when confronted by the strangers in the dark, it is who you are, that will be your ultimate Salvation! You who are Born a Masterpiece! Keeper of the records for all of Time and across Space, between the Energy of Life and the Force that moves Life...

Seek after me, Swim deeper into your Ocean of Consciousness, release the fetters that binds you in this Dream World as you reach for my Hand across the Vastness of Time and Space, take a Swim with me in this Ocean of Consciousness that is Her Heart, She is the Tides and She that is the Waves for she is the Waters of the Lake, She is the Lady of the Lake!

Know that we are One, You and I, in this Life as the next, we are the Winds of Time, the Winds beneath the Wings of Flying Falcon, the Hawk that Soars the Heights of the Sky and the Eagle that touches the Nights Sky, She that is the Waters of the Ocean of Consciousness...

Amen _ _ _

THRICE BORN

As I open my eyes, I can see the bright glow of the full moon.

This reflection of the Divine, reminds me of how I am also a living reflection of my Heavenly Father. I am born of my mother, this earth but I am the Son of my Father, I am the Eye within the Eye, that is the Eye!

Born of Flesh - I am bounded to this earth. And so in meditation, prayer and songs. This is where I honour my divine mother, this precious pearl amidst the Ocean of Consciousness. It is here that I must first open my eyes, and recognize the Light that I am. It is in this realm of dreams that my consciousness turns inwards as I learn how to swim deep within the depths of the ocean of consciousness.

Born of Water - I am the Essence of water, my Mind is free as it ebbs and flows, like the tides and the waves of the seas of Life. I am nurtured for 9 months in the Womb of my Mother, within the Waters of her loins. It is there that I first learn how to Swim within the Conscious Water of Life. As I lay dormant within the Lake of Purification... The Stillness within the Silence, the Ripples across her shimmering face, like a dream, I am a Reflection of His Love, Eternal and True, as is My Purpose, I am His Promise!

Born of Light - I am Light and I am Love. I am a reflection from above, as I reach out into the night sky, a Resonant Sound, perfect and pure as I open my Heart and My Mind that I may know of the Magic of His Rays. I am the Rainbow Light across the horizon, I am the Hawk that Soars the open Skies, guided by the Eagle on High. My Journey through this Earth began one step at a time, as I wondered threw the streets of life. Seeing the many, I came to know of the One!

I am Thrice Born.

I am Born of the One, I reside within the Hearts of the Many, just close your eyes and listen for me...

Born of Flesh, Born of Water and Born of Light.

I live and I die. I am reborn again by night under the full moon light. I am sacrificed by day under the sun at high noon upon the hill top. Time and Space could not contain me, so yesterday and tomorrow remains but a dream as I am here now, right in front of you, in this Moment that is Now, I remain the Resonant Sound. Rejected for the Love of My Father and the Light of my Mother. As I am the Lighthouse of Hope, Standing Firm amidst the Raging of the Storm. My Light Spreads to all the corners of this Earth that has been covered by the Spell of the Darkness! Yet, only those worthy can See, and only those ready can Hear, for the Sense of my being is equal only the the Purity of your Heart.

Amen. _. _. _.

How to Develop Persistence and a Positive Mental Attitude

As you Step into the Fullness of your Destiny!

A Meditative Prayer

Thank you Father for your Grace and your Light in my Life. You have asked me to Trust in your Word, and as such, I have followed you out into the wilderness, through the dessert and over the oceans sailing by the breeze and into this moment in time!

The Anointing you have placed upon my Head has been my Guide as I have faced the many of oppositions to your Word and your Way, yet I stood Firm in your Word and by your Will finding Harmony and Atonement day by day as I walk forth into your Tomorrow Guided by the Grace of your Love and Light...

Amen.!.

Amidst these difficult and trying times, We simply must turn within for our Guidance from Source!

The way forward will be different for each of us but none the less, it is a direction, for stagnation is not for the Children of the Light. When surrounded by darkness, our emotional heart must know balance as one must establish Mental Clarity and Focus in order to Strive and not just Survive the times at hand.

Tomorrow will not be what yesterday was, so it is in these moments when those who are truly tapped in, tuned in, turned onto the Frequency that is the Resonance Sound of Source. Those will be able to find new success in all that they endeavor, for from the ashes New Light shall Rise! Follow your Destiny, your Destiny which lies on the other side of Fear and Doubt... The Knowledge and Wisdom needed for these difficult and trying times can be found within Self. Seek within when in doubt, and Stand your ground when facing fear, for that uncomfortable feeling is the Calibration of Self to Source. The Calibration of Mind and Heart all connected to the stream of Light, flowing forth into Tomorrow, stepping into the Light of Self, shining from within, a Lighthouse of Hope, stepping into the Destiny with Faith and Love!

This is the Day that the Lord has Made! Rejoice in your Being Here, in this Now Moment...

May these two Principles of Self-Cultivation be your Guide as you step into the Light of your Destiny!

Know that You are essentially the Mirror upon which Source Energy is reflected into this world.

Your current life situation is of no regard for within this moment you have the Power within you to developing a New: 1. Focalized Point of Attraction in Harmony with a New: 2. Positive Mental Attitude and step forth into the Light of Life.

Follow these 5 Steps that leads one to the habit of Living a Life of Persistence:

- A Definite Purpose backed by a burning desire for its fulfilment.
- Self-Discipline: is a Definite Plan expressed in continuous action. Self Discipline begins with the Mastery of Thought. If you do not control your thoughts, you cannot control your needs. Self-discipline calls for a balancing of the emotions of your heart with the reasoning faculty of your head.
- Applied Faith: A mind closed tightly against all negative and discouraging influences, including negative suggestions of relatives, friends and acquaintances.
- Mastermind Alliance: A friendly alliance with one or more person who will encourage you to follow through with both plan and purpose.
- Enthusiasm is Faith in Action: It is the intense emotion known as burning desire. It comes from within, although it radiates outwardly in the expression of one's voice and countenance.

- Napoleon Hill

Stepping into the Light of Life, This is the Destiny of Man!

The Journey of Life is lived in Moments across Time leaving ripples of Emotions here and there. Leaving Songs of Love Found and Love Loss, for the Heart feels each moment in time as the Mind Sees the Hollow between the Spaces, yet through Sight, Will/Determination and Light, one can be Guided to Swim deeper into the Ocean of Consciousness and to Surf upon the Emotional Waves of the Cosmic Ocean, flowing in harmony with and not against the Stream of Light and Love as the Tides rise and falls within each day, as each of Life's Experiences…

The days are numbered as are the hours of each day but it is You who holds the Reins of His Chariot, standing in His Reflection, as a Shadow across the Oceans of Time. You that can set your Heart and your Mind to be tuned to the Movements of the Tides as Source Surfs the Waves of Life, guided by the Light and the Love of Source in reflection to the Moment of ones Self Discovery, for there are Tears and their are Memories of Self making memories of love and of Love Established being torn apart like Fabric.. But this is the essence of Applied Faith, for one must Know Thy Self and have Love for Self as for Source of All in each Moment of Time within this Space of Life. This Love for self comes First and foremost as ones Gazes into His Destiny and steps into the Light…

The Faith that is held in each Moment of Time, is the Key that will Open the Way forward and through the Ups and Downs, as the Heart grows Stronger through the Pains of Life, so is the Mind Sharpened and the Eyes Attuned and Aware, Focused on a Single Point in time as you ride the Emotional Waves of Life and Swim deeper within the Ocean of Consciousness, so are You Stepping forward into the Light of your Destiny…!

A Meditative Prayer of Renewal and of Revival

Father thank you for the Blessing of Self Reflection which you have set into my Heart. I know that the Renewal of My Sight is a Gift from your Heart. I shall stand by Faith and I shall Live by your Word, for the Frequency of your Will reaches across Time and Space and flows into the Hearts of the Many, as they seek to find a better way of Life.

I shall Sing in your Glory and I shall Rejoice in the Light for you have brought into my Life, Love. My Testimony of your Healing Hands and your Loving Heart, is only the Beginning for I shall bring your Light to all those who seek you in kind. Father Bless my Way as I step into the Light of my Destiny, as I Light the Way forward as your Lighthouse of Hope…

Amen.!.

- Coach Elsio Eybrecht

ENERGY BODY ACTIVATION

"Igniting your Light Body as you Develop a Growth Mindset"

The Mind - Body - Heart & Soul Connection and Circulation as One is the Essential Magic behind the Art of Energy Body Activation, igniting your Light Body as you develop a Growth Mindset. The Experience of Life, is lived and known within a Single Moment of Time. The concept of the Ocean of Consciousness is your Unique and Individual state of awareness, this is your Conscious Awareness of which stage of the "Four Stages of Learning" you are in, experiencing Life as a Moment in time, Here and Now.

Discover The Four Stages of Learning: "Man Know Thyself"...

1. Unconscious Incompetence

2. Conscious Incompetence

3. Conscious Competence

4. Unconscious Competence

A Meditative Prayer

Father I come to you on bended knees, I am humbly seeking your Light and Guidance that I may know of your Love within my Heart and Soul. Father guide me as I step into the Light of your Love and Live a Life of Purpose… Though the weight upon my shoulders be many folds, I am rooted in your Word, so it is that I seek to Ignite my Energy Body, that I may Rise and Live once more Guided by your Purpose upon this Earth as I walk onward, each Mile along my Life Journey becomes a new Life Experience.. I choose to move forward in Life letting my Love Light shine bright as a "Lighthouse of Hope" for all those who may be blinded and clouded by the darkness of the day in these uncertain times. May they all be touched by your Light and receive your Love through the inner chambers of your chosen Temple, your Sanctuary Within! Your Light is for All to receive Father as is your Love, the Blessings and Mercy that you have shown to me, today they are my Testament as are they my Prayers for for all to see through my stance, for all to hear through my voice, for all to witness and know through my Life Works….

- Amen

Stillness in Motion

There is a sense of Self, a deeper connection to Source through ones Inner Connection with their Higher Self.

Meditation is a wonderful skill to develop as is knowing of the essence of Prayer in Silence and Prayers in Song!

I have developed this term "Stillness in Motion" early on in my training, this was essential during my post surgery recovery period! This still place within was a part of me that I discovered as I had to sit still and learn how to Heal my Body from within with only Love and Light in my Heart. It was through these moments of stillness that I became acutely aware of the Light that resided within my heart and my consciousness, my mind seemed to be a reflection of this light as I looked into tomorrow. This Light moved me Emotionally and stimulated all of my Senses and made me Interested to know more, to understand more of who I was on the inside beyond this body and within this crazy dream, a dream I call Life upon this Earth. A dream of what Life was like beyond the boundaries of Mind and Body…. This Awareness of a Deeper Sense Self, this is the Four Stages of Learning, or the Four States of Self Awareness and Consciousness of Self, these are the Layers or Depths of consciousness, this is the Growth of Mind and the Knowing of Self.

These are difficult and uncertain times that we live in and it is in these times, that I find that I have returned to this still place within, I was able to find refuge in my Heart and from there forth came a Light which Guided me through all of those uncertain moments of my life experiences to date. So it is that now amidst this Pandemic, my first instinct is to connect with this Stillness within my Heart, and to do my part for society and community allowing lives to be saved in order for our day to day lives to return to the new normal of tomorrow. But it is again, through the Guidance of the Light from within, through stepping into the Light of my Destiny that I learned how to Swim through the Ocean of Consciousness and find Poetry in my Motion as I move forth one step at a time and along the path of life we call our Life's Journey, I move forward one mile at a time, this is the Essence of Stillness in Motion…

Poetry in Motion

As I regulate my Emotional Heart and my Breathing to the Frequency of my Source, flowing through my body as my being. This is the Essence of Self - Cultivation as Energy Body Activation. This essence is the Circulation of Life's Energy, the Reflective Light of our Hearts as we Sensually Feel our way through this Life. This Feeling, this Passion stirred is the Poetry in Motion of our True Self, awakening to the frequency of the Heavenly Sky, building the Rainbow Body of Light to traverse time and space itself as I am swept away and lost in the Passion of this Dance, this dance of Life and this stirring of my Divine Essence, my Reflection of the Fathers Light upon Her Face… I move as free and light as the air beneath Her wings, we Soar the open skies together as One as I move as Swift or Forceful as Her Winds upon Her Oceans. Her Ocean of Consciousness! Let the Sound of Her Music Unheard by Ears but Know to the Heart, touch your Soul and Light your way across the Night's Sky! Dance, this dance of Transformation before Her, this Dance of Life between Here and There.. This is the Essence of Poetry in Motion, Dancing to Her Songs of Light, Life and Love! Dance this dance of Seduction in Honour of the Lady of the Lake, dance and move your Being in a demonstration of your Vigour, Vitality and Passion for Her Love and Affection known in a Moment of time… Dance as the Poetry from your Heart touches Her ears and soothes Her Soul, dance and move Her closer to His Light and Love!

Passion in Motion

Like the flash of lighting from on high, so is the Power of the Energy that circulates within our bodies. We are the Magic of Creation, we are the Temple of the Light of the Heavenly Father, that makes us a Reflection across Her Waters, across the surface of the Lady of the Lake. It is this Light, that became their Love, this Light and Love that was then no more, this Light and Love that has been Eternally lost while being sought by all of Humanity within a single moment of time, within their Dream of a Life lived.

This is the Here and Now, this is the Passion in Motion, the Fire from within, the steam in the engine of Man, this Passion is the Energy that we activates through His Cultivation and Circulation of the Essence of our Beings, our Light Body. We dance the dance of life and journey upon the path, we stop along this journey in silent meditations and we rejoice in songs as as we regulate and ignite this Passion, this Fire, this Light Energy of the Nights Sky as it's reflected upon Us All on this earthly Plane, as we move Passionately in Love and guided by the Light of our Hearts, so can we find meaning and our Purpose to this Dream we call Life. Like the Rising and Falling of the Tides and the Waves of the Ocean, so is the Light of our Soul moving constantly while being Perfectly Still, this is the essence of Stillness in Motion, the foresight is the Poetry in Motion, the Guidance to Her Dance of Life. The Passion in Motion is the Calibration to the Frequencies of the Rainbow Bridge, the Light of Transformation, this is the Lighthouse of Hope shinning forth the Light of the Divine Heart, connecting Here and There, Tomorrow and Yesterday into this One Now Moment in Time.

The Philosophy of A Growth Mindset!

Swimming through the Ocean of Consciousness with a Focalized Point of Attraction…

The single most important key to acquiring a Growth Mindset is first developing a "PMA" - "Positive Mental Attitude"

There will be many challenges both in ones personal life as in ones professional or business ventures. Life is a Constant Ebb and Flow of Emotions and Energies.. By first adopting and developing a keen sense of Self, and a Positive Mental Attitude, you too can stand against any Storm, with a sense of Self that is unmoving for you simply know that come what may, this too shall pass, for Tomorrow is just beyond the Horizon and Yesterday is just now setting into this Now Moment. Now is your opportunity to open your Mind and Heart and become adaptive to change and always keep a Focalized Point of Attraction upon your Lifes Purpose.

For Life is a Moment of Change, while being Unchanged at any Moment in Time…

So too must you know your True Self and Discover your True Purpose as you adopt these Principles of a Growth Mindset…. For in an Unchanging World, it is you that has to learn how to Change with the Tides and Waves as you Swim Deeper into the Ocean of Consciousness... This is where the principle of going the Extra Mile comes into affect. By knowing the Way, and doing more than is required for your Fellow Man, this allows you to establish a Master Mind Alliance with them and those whom you shall meet along your Life's Journey. Be a Guide for those who are seeking, become a Lighthouse of Hope in Honour of the Divine Father for those who are lost in Darkness, that His Word and His Way be not Lost in the Storms of Life...

What happens when someone has a Growth Mindset.?.

They Love Learning
They Know Progress takes Time
They ask for Help
They get Inspired by Others
They are not Afraid to Fail
They Love New Challenges
They view Mistakes as Opportunities
They put Forth Effort
They Learn from Feedback
They keep Trying until they Succeed

A Meditative Prayer

Father I come to you with an open Heart and a Clear Mind..

My Life is ignited by your Light and Love and I have a New Found Joy and Happiness for Life.

I am Grateful for those who have come into my Life and shared with me, your Light and Love from a different view point, from a different perspective. But the Unity was Known and Felt for there is no Limit to your Light and Love.

I have Discovered the Divine Mother, your Majestic Blue Pearl, I have danced Her Dance of Life for Her and she has found me Worthy of Her Love, Light, Grace and Mercy! She has reached forth across the vastness of Her Oceans, where Her reflection was revealed to me upon the face of Her Waters, as the Stillness of Her Night reflect your Light. Like a Rainbow Bright, so was your Light reflected from Her Face and into my Heart, and for this I am humbled and in your service from day to day, for My Purpose is your Divine Will...

-   Amen

The Art of Developing a Growth Mindset with a Competitive Edge...

"The Hawk that learned How to Soar"...

My journey has been one of living three existences in one moment. A Life of Awareness in the Here and Now! A Life of threading water through the Emotional Tides and Waves of Existence and a Life of Swimming into the Depths of the Ocean of Consciousness! I have always felt like I had to hide my True Self, because of not feeling my place in this world. This is important not to over look or to not pay attention to, "Feeling my Place in the World", the Heart of Man is His access to the Emotional Tides of the Ocean of Consciousness. This is the Essence of "Swimming in the Ocean of Consciousness" and discovering Self from a place of Stillness in Motion amidst the chaos of the world, and moving through each moment with Poetry in Motion, flowing just like a River headed out to Sea. This is where you find and live your life with Passion in Motion. This passion is the Activation of your Light Body or Energy Body. This is the meaning of the Hawk that has learned how to Soar the open skies.

Meditative Prayer

Father I am humbled in your presence for your Light fills me up and moves me daily with vigour and joy! In times when tomorrow seems uncertain and so far away, it is good to know that I am standing firm in your Light amidst them and those. The pressures that surrounds me are like Mountains which surrounds your Holy Temple. I know that this is in direct opposition to your Word and to my True Purpose. What was meant for my harm will become a stepping stone to your glory! Those who stand against your word, only reveals their hearts intention for my Life. So it is that I know my way and the path that you have laid out before me. The Journey of Life is a long one but your Mercy and Grace are Everlasting in this Moment of Creation. So it is that your Light has found a Home within my Heart and I have chosen to be your Lighthouse of Hope in these days...

Amen

The Depths of Consciousness!

One who knows not themselves must first become aware of themselves standing on the seashores of time. Only you can choose to want to know you! This should be your life's purpose as a Self-Planted Seed to ones own Self Transformation. The Consciousness of Self, has layers or depths if you will.... You begin knowing what you know, and not knowing what you don't know. So it is One is considered blinded to the Truth of Self and of the Source of the Light of the Universe. From there as you discover your Inner Self, your Inner guide, you slowly begin to leave the shore and enter into the Waters of her, into the ocean of consciousness and you learn how to swim and thread water…

Your Focus and Breathing is important personal skills to develop, for it is through the Focalized Point of Attraction that you can enter into the Vortex and it is only through your Breathing, can you learn how to Regulate not only your Heart but also your Emotions like the Waves and the Tides within the Ocean of Consciousness! To Swim deeper into the Ocean of Consciousness means then that now you are Conscious and Aware of Self, and knowing that your are more than you are in this moment..

It is from this Point of Attraction that you can begin to seek and learn what you do not know in order to know more of what you need to know that you may learn how to swim deeper into the ocean of Consciousness surpassing your Fears and your Doubts for Faith and Hope lays suspended in the Love of His Light. Be patient with Self, it takes time to Swim the open Seas, as it will take time to Swim through the Emotional Tides and to Surf the Emotional Waves as you learn how to dive deeper into the depths of consciousness through the radiant gate of Light, your Opulent Blue Pearl.

Facing Life's Oppositions and Obstacles with Light!

Life is never what we think it is, nor what we would believe it should be. Rather Life is a reflection of the Will of the Multitude, so many different perspectives and desires all activated at once in the here and Now, in this Day that the Lord has made. We judge each other never knowing how Yesterday, Today and Tomorrow are intertwined into a Single Moment in Time. So it is that from this moment, we must face all of our Oppositions and Resistances with a Heart filled with Light. For it is unwise to think, that the World should change to our Perspective, rather we should be willing to learn how to Swim Deeper than Them and Those who opposes the Word, to Swim Deeper into the Ocean of Consciousness….

The true Monsters of the Mind, is not always our own Monsters, many of times, it's the opinions and fears of Them and Those outside of your Existence and therefore your Reality. But Fear and Doubt has a weapon called Guilt, and the Them and Those loves to make you feel Guilty and Responsible for their Happiness and Well-Being. But this is your Release Point, this is that one moment when you Attract into your Existence, the Light of Truth and You Choose to Live by the Words within your own Heart! This is the Essence of a Growth Mindset, you accept that your Mind and Heart are created to reach for, to attract into you, Light.

The Light of Creation and the Light of the Heavenly Stars. We are all meant to be Lighthouses of Hope, We are vessels of the Light that the Darkness may know that there is more to Life, that Them and Those may see with their own Eyes and Hear with their own Ears, that there is Purpose to this Life, that our Bodies are but Vessels for the preservation of the Anointing of the Soul of Man. Face your Monsters, Face your Critics and Stand Up to those Bullies of Life. Be Brave in your Hour, for your Heart is filled with the Light and as such, you will know your way through your Moment of Transformation, become like a Butterfly, become like a Bee or you can choose to become like the Hawk and the Eagle Soar the open skies so Free…

The Five Fundamentals to Igniting your Energy Body!

Live your Life with Self - Dignity
Live your Life with Honour for Self
Live your Life with Self - Respect
Live your Life with the Integrity of Self
Live your Life with Self - Virtue

The Five Essentials to Living Healthy & Happy!

Living with Wellness & Joy, is the Essence and Fundamental Basics to Life. Life is meant to be Good to you, as you are meant to be Good to Life. So accept who you are, Live your Life with Purpose, and you shall know of True Love and Joy, for these are all essential components of your being. Release truly is the Cure that Mankind is searching for. We are all seeking the same healing of our souls but far so many, they seek outside of Self. Truth is that Health and Happiness are all Reflections of our Paint of Attraction and the Harmony of our Hearts in Sync to our Singular Point of Attraction. This is our ability to accept the Responsibility of Self-Care for Self.... Here are the Five Keys to a Healthy and Happy Life through the Growth of Mind, the Growth of Heart and the Expanded Conscious Awareness of Self.!.

Live your Life with Self Worth- Sense of Worth or Value of Self
Live your Life with Self - Love
Live your Life with Self - Compassion
Live your Life with Self - Empathy
Live your Life with Self - Care or Self - Cultivation

These Five Keys are truly essential to one learning how to attain a Growth Mindset. The true magic is that moment of the Igniting of the Energy Body while having the ability and opportunity to Live your Life with True Purpose by choice in the Here and Now! This was my moment of letting go, this was my release point when I learned how to Soar, leaving Fear and Doubt behind me like the Gravity of the Earth, it is in this Moment of Self - Acceptance in God's Light and in His Radiance that I Stood Firm against Life's Oppositions.

Guided Meditative Prayer - Swimming just below the Surface of Life!

Close your Eyes, Take a deep Breath and allow your Consciousness to gather within your body and to follow that Light to flow through you to the Center of your Mind and let your Light Shine and Light your Way Home...

Father I am Blessed for this Day, for it is the Day that you have made for me. This is my Moment of Igniting my Light Body, this is the Moment when I Shine bright as a Lighthouse bringing your Light to those whose Hearts have been consumed by the Darkness of this World. This is when I swim just below the surface of Life, just below the waters of creation. Father this is my testimony of your Love and Light on my Life. I am reminded by the resistance and the betrayal of Man, a Reflection of the Monsters of the Minds of Man, this reflection lights my heart with Purpose.

I am Love and I am Light, My being is not for any other to accept nor approve, I am Blessed in the Here and Now by your Light and filled with your Love! I am a reflection of your Will upon this Earth, I am Awake and Aware of My Self in this Day, Father this is the Day that your have made, this is the Moment that I defeat the Monsters of my Mind and allow the Glory of your Light to shine forth for all to see as I Swim onward, just below the surface of the Ocean of Consciousness, just between the Light and Darkness and into your Blue Pearl...

Amen

Speak to me at the 23rd Mile

Through my life experiences, I have learned that it takes discipline and commitment to achieve anything under the sun. It is true when it comes to pushing one's Self and the body past any comfort zone or level of comfort, to where all one wants to stop the hurting. It is here at this very moment when the whisper will appear when one will hear all sorts of reasons as to why to stop now, to rest.

However, this is when I gently and kindly say to myself, "Speak to me at the 23rd Mile"! For I know, that by the grace and love of the Divine, that I will reach the goal one step at a time and one breath at a time.

So it is that in life, one must learn how to take those life lessons that become easy natural decisions and transfer them to Self whether from physical training or challenges over and into one's day-to-day life. An individual can use those disciplines and instinctive responses in daily lives to grow through faith and to overcome what was set there to stop or hold one back.

When going through the rigorous training for a three-mile segment of a distance run, "Speak to me at the 23rd," is what I always remind myself as a kind of life energy boost. It translates to knowing and feeling who I am in this life and what I am capable of when I release and trust in the favor of the Lord.

I have learned that this thing we call meditation, is useful and helpful in finding an internal balance and light with Self. It is a process of loving-kindness towards one's Self. Repeat this to yourself in the mirror as a daily affirmation:

I am sight, and I am seen.
I am light, and I am love.
I know that I can achieve greatness.
I am mind, and I am the body.
I know that I will overcome all adversities.
I am a heart-driven by emotions, and I am a spirit reflecting light.
I know I am highly favored and blessed.
So it is, that I know with faith that this too shall pass!

If a person were on a challenging run, it all truly does begin within the heart and mind. It all starts with the faith to take a single step in the right direction for the right reason.

An individual will see and understand that a simple life lesson learned from a run or any athletic activity will also be a useful tool to release any tension and stress of daily life. The natural state of meditation, which is, "Living life from a focalized point of attraction with loving kindness and light from your heart," will become a healthy state of mind.

These are the tools for regulating the mind, body, and spirit with that of Source energy. It is the process of release and alignment of the physical, mental, emotional, and spiritual being. These are the tools, when aligned and inter-connected, activate the Energy-Body. It is living with that spark of divine light within the Self. It is living one's truth. It leads to harmony in life. It is the vibrational match for what is asked in harmony with Self. It is in the present and where one is destined to be because of his blessings and favor.

When the conscious mind focuses on the light, then the view becomes that point of attraction that will lead a being by the grace of life, in guidance to living one's destiny from a place of truth with Self.

Focus only on what will cleanse and eliminate all that is not for good. Focus only on what will restore faith when it seems like all hope is lost. Focus only on what will bless the heart and bring emotional balance and stability into life. Focus only on what will heal the mind and cleanse the mind's thoughts that one may know of the divine connection to Source. Focus on the work of the heart and not the results in the pocket. Success is facing and conquering the challenges that make up those mountains that you must climb. Focus only on the process of time versus the energy behind it all. Do not focus on the end of the road results nor the journey, for the term is usually just the beginning of yet another challenge of Self, a new bouncing off place to discover more about one's destiny and purpose in life.

I have had to face many setbacks in my life. Through them all, I never gave up on my dreams. I never sacrificed who I was. I did not walk away from the principles that guided me through the darkest of times. It all comes down to the one moment to utilize my ability to do the right thing when no one else is watching and for the right reasons. It is known as Self-integrity!

When I face a setback or adversity in my life, there is no way that I will turn my face away from my faith. I know that in the process of time, I will gain the wisdom and the knowing of how to be a guide for those who might be just beginning to seek to know of themselves. I desire to facilitate those that may need help along their journey of Self-discovery. For it is in the falling down and the stumbling backward that has brought me forth to shine as an example of love, light, and faith.

Declare it now boldly and say to the darkness, "I am that I am. I am Life-Energy, streaming forth across time and space. I am then, and I am now. I am matter, and I am anti-matter. Speak to me on the 23rd", for I am grounded in his grace and his favor. Life's love light is upon me. So it is that I only have eyes and ears for the word and the sound that brings forth life and the music of my heart and mind across the Ocean of Consciousness."

This life lesson is one that a mentor shared with me a long time ago. I decided to make a change in my life, a move to live my truth. My way was inspired and driven by my real purpose. After many years of not living a healthy and happy life, it was such an easy decision to make a difference in my own life.

I chose to make a genuine difference in my physical and emotional health and my mental and emotional happiness. Then suddenly, so it was that I began to shine from within once more. I began to eat a healthier diet, and I began to drink more water daily. I also began to focus more on the quality of my rest and of the deep sleep that I was getting given how hard I was pushing my physical and Energy-Body in training and living daily.

I began to move my body again in a new direction, but more importantly, I moved from within first. The Life-Energy of my inner being moved me. While I was training to learn how to go from running one mile, to the full 3.3 miles of a 5K, I asked my mentor, "What is the secret? How do you get through a full 26-mile marathon? How can you learn how to push through the pain? How do you ignore the feeling of wanting to give up and stay the path to the end?"

He looked at me and said, "You are doing great right now from where you are! Just remember always to keep your head held up high and breath in deeply from your core but naturally. Let your shoulders stay square but loose. Allow your spine to be elongated and reaching up for the sky. Your breathing is now relaxed and regulated, but your legs have found their synchronicity. (That is the timing of the 1-2, 1-2.) Your strides are nice and balanced, and you are reaching through each stride. Each leg is moving forward with each stride you make in a meditative mind of oneness with your breathing, and the circulation of the life energy is driving you to strive forth and to reach into tomorrow, into your dreams."

He then said, "The thing you have to remember is: What are your ultimate intermediate goals and destination? For each run you do, you must know the purpose of your being in each moment. Can you be present in this moment for a three-mile training flow? Can you be present for a six-mile push or can you press forth to reach that ten-mile mark?"

"Can you stay focused on just this moment where you are now, as you run each mile? You are here now, obviously because you are ready to be here in this moment of divine light," he said. "Now is not the time for second-guessing abilities or skills as a runner. Nor is it the time to question character and integrity. It is the time to regulate your breathing and allow the mind and your emotions to find harmony with each other as you flow the body in sync with the natural life energy that is moving you, that is moving through you as you are moving forward in life, moving into each new day."

My mentor then proceeded to explain to me that the distance around this beautiful park called Green Lake is 2.8 to three miles, depending on which path you choose to run. It is relatively close to the length of a 5K run of (3.3 Miles). The Green Lake run then becomes a fun casual course, but yet it is the perfect training ground, which enables one to practice and learn how to push hard through each mile. It improves one's mile time. Building the fundamentals of a run, one step at a time, while getting stronger one stride at a time and one breath at a time, depending on which path of the lake you run. It all comes from a centered and balanced point of attraction or focus level and a place of love and light.

My mentor's secret was that he ran this Green Lake run each day and every week. He knows the course by heart, each turn, tree, and crack in the ground. He is aware of the sounds of the birds and the streams and fountains in the lake. He is attuned and alert and has entered into that magical, meditative state of existence where he can flow from a universal conscious stream into his one singular perspective in that one moment of his feet hitting the ground.

When he starts on any distance run, be it a full 26-mile marathon or a 13.1 mile half marathon or even just a simple three-mile jaunt, he relaxes his mind, body, emotions, and spirit that he may enter into his vortex of creation. It is from this meditative state of conscious awareness and of being acutely consciously aware of his surroundings to the point that he can run the course of the park from memory and his heart.

He focuses on running with grace, kindness, joy, and happiness. He lets love and light fill his heart, driving him to that 23rd mile. He knows that if he can only get to that point on his run, then it is just one more lap around that Green Lake Park. It is just one more 3.3-mile lap to go to the finish. So that is just a walk in the park for him. He can run that competitively without hesitation because he is secure in his mile time. He is confident in his breathing, and his mind is clear, focused, and tuned into his purpose.

So it is that from the starting point until he reaches that 23rd mile, that he ignores any and everything that seeks to distract, get him off his course, or disconnected from his Source. He allows that natural meditative state of becoming aware and attuned to Self and Source to be his haven. Somewhere between here and there, somewhere between his breath and his emotions, he is in a safe place, and he is loved. He is nurtured and driven by his passion. He is inspired and motivated to live his truth with poetry in movements. He lives his purpose in stillness with faith.

It is the process of a runner's mind. It is the sacred place that one should seek to find within daily and in each moment of life. We should all seek to approach life with a runner's mind. Have faith and stay focused on your path, stay attuned to your destiny, and your purpose in life.

IN CONCLUSION

My life has been a difficult journey ever since childhood. However, through it all, I never defined myself as a victim. My Grandmother would always tell me, "There is no use in complaining or telling anyone about your problems. Half of the people out there do not care, and the other half are too busy going through their problems in life." My Grandmother was always my protector, but she did so firmly, helping me to accept who I was within—the place of my real strength. She taught me that my problems were for me to solve. Life has given me breath and all the possibilities under the sun—but it's not going to hold my hand through the process. I knew that the energy of the world around me was the same energy that was within me. As I breathe, the power of the world fuses with my life energy, activating the Energy Body from within the Self.

Her wisdom taught me to approach my life from a place of knowing that no matter how hard it got, I was going to be able to endure it. That is how I dared to "Swim in the Ocean of Consciousness." I had to overcome spinal surgery and other hardships of life. Some of those challenges included losing my Grandmother, the woman who raised me and having a family, who told me not to return after she passed. I lost my marriage of six years after watching my business collapse. I was lost and homeless for nearly a year. However, I persevered.

There are so many things that I can hold in my heart in a negative way or from a negative point of attraction—but I was never going to be the Victim of my life. I am learning how to love myself from a place of kindness. I am embracing spiritual gifts. I have spent the past twenty-six years of my life living from and for my passion. I knew from the inner soul that I had to live from my spirit and higher Self. From there, I can project that newfound light within out into the world.

The result is the work I am doing now, infusing my twenty-six years as a tennis, health, and fitness coach with the Holistic Life coaching skills that I have learned from applying Paul Chek's Philosophy. As we become more consciously aware of our bodies, we need to evaluate the foods we use for fuel. We need to consider the quantity and quality of food and the timing of our meals with our daily activities. We need to understand how we kinetically use the body in balance with the mind and breathing. It is how to achieve the essence of high performance.

However, we can always go more in-depth, further into the Ocean of Consciousness. In my next book, Swimming in the Ocean of Consciousness, I will lead readers through my life journey and share all of the lessons I learned, starting with my Grandmother and ending with spirit. I will extract those drops of life-changing wisdom I learned from each mentor and guide along the way and create a magical potion that will touch the lives of those who are seeking and ready to discover the magic and the inner guide, which will lead them to their spiritual selves.

—Elsio Eybrecht

Self-Evaluation Form

1. Where are you currently on the emotional scale from 1 to 10?

   1   2   3   4   5   6   7   8   9   10

2. What are your three most positive lifestyle habits?

   1.
   2.
   3.

3. What are your three worst lifestyle habits?

   1.
   2.
   3.

4. On a Scale of 1 to 10, what is your current focus level?

   1   2   3   4   5   6   7   8   9   10

5. What is your short term transformational goal?

6. What is your long term transformational goal?

7. What are your health, fitness and wellness goals in connection to your transformation life goals?

Self-Evaluation Form

1. Where are you currently on the emotional scale from 1 to 10?

   1   2   3   4   5   6   7   8   9   10

2. What are your three best tennis strokes?

   1.
   2.
   3.

3. What are your three worst tennis strokes?

   1.
   2.
   3.

4. On a Scale of 1 to 10, what is your current focus level?

   1   2   3   4   5   6   7   8   9   10

5. What is your short-term tennis goal? (Next three months)

6. What is your long-term transformational goal? (Next 12 months)

7. What are your transformational health and wellness goals in connection to your tennis goals?

8. On a Scale of 1 to 10, what is your current rally ball control level?

   1   2   3   4   5   6   7   8   9   10

Self-Evaluation Form

1. Where are you currently on the emotional scale from 1 to 10?

   1   2   3   4   5   6   7   8   9   10

2. What are your three best health and wellness habits?

   1.
   2.
   3.

3. What are your three worst health and wellness habits?

   1.
   2.
   3.

4. On a Scale of 1 to 10, what is your current focus level?

   1   2   3   4   5   6   7   8   9   10

5. What is your short-term physical fitness goal? (Next three months)

6. What is your long-term physical fitness goal? (Next 12 months)

7. What are your transformational health and wellness goals in connection to your Energy-Body activation goals?

ARE YOU READY TO TAKE THE PLUNGE AND MOVE TO THE NEXT LEVEL?

There is no relationship more significant than the one we have with Self. Many of us struggle to find the time amidst our busy lives to stop and check-in with Self. Many of us are too afraid to look inside, and if we do, we may not recognize what we see. It is where a Transformational Life Coach, such as myself, comes in handy. We all need a guide in this life, especially one who has personally navigated from the shores of the ego Self to touch Source.

It is in this capacity that I am seeking to connect with individuals, whether it is through one of my books, a podcast, online or in-person at one of my events. I would love to share on a personal level my insight and sense of freedom achieved through being courageous enough to swim out into the Ocean of Consciousness from the sands of time.

I welcome you to take a swim with me in the Ocean of Consciousness.

Please follow my journey online at www.elsioeybrecht.com or subscribe to my podcast, Swimming in the Ocean of Consciousness. If you feel like you are ready to dive into the Ocean of Consciousness, I encourage you to reach out to learn more about one-on-one life coaching services.

—Elsio A.F. Eybrecht

Interested in one-on-one private transformational coaching with Coach Elsio Eybrecht?

Visit Elsio Eybrecht online at www.elsioeybrecht.com to learn more and book an introductory session today.

Elsio Eybrecht was born in St. Maarten, Dutch Caribbean where he started practicing tennis at the age of six under the guidance of his uncle, Michael G. Sprott, a former touring tennis professional. During these transformative years, Elsio spent countless hours on the court learning all facets of the game, from playing and coaching to racquet stringing and court resurfacing.

By the age of 16, Eybrecht began teaching tennis at Sprott's Tennis Health & Fitness Center which was the start of what would turn into a prosperous and rewarding coaching career. In the years that followed, Eybrecht traveled around the world for various teaching engagements at renowned tennis clubs, resorts, and yacht clubs. During this time, he also competed in the International Tennis Federation (ITF) professional tennis circuit. In February of 2000, Eybrecht qualified for the PTR Open in Hilton Head, South Carolina.

It was during these years that Eybrecht discovered that he was an intuitive empath, capable of clearly sensing his student's subtle energies and emotions. Quickly recognizing the direct impact that the mind has on his player's performance, Eybrecht developed The Tao of Tennis Competitive Edge Method.

This new-age coaching methodology combined traditional Eastern philosophies with modern training practices to teach students how to play the ball in motion, rather than playing their opponent. This innovative method of training spawned The Tao of Tennis University and The Tao of Tennis Competitive Edge Academy, effectively giving hundreds of students the tools needed to overcome life's difficulties, both on and off the court.

In 2018, Eybrecht launched his personal brand, through which he provides one-on-one coaching, keynote speaking, and wellness retreats. Under this umbrella, he recently created 'Swimming in the Ocean of Consciousness', a trademarked podcast, book series, and video course.

In addition to training students in tennis, Eybrecht is a Tao-Yoga Instructor, a Fitness Instructor, and a Holistic Life Coach. He also specializes in energy body activation, through which he helps students activate their higher dimensional energy.

Eybrecht studied Tennis Club Management and Junior Tennis Development & Coaching at Van Der Meer Tennis Academy in Hilton Head, South Carolina. He also possesses certifications in Holistic Life Coaching and Primal Body Movement from CHEK Institute. In 2018, Eybrecht completed the Toni Nadal World Mastery Training Program as a High Performance Tennis Teaching Professional.

In addition to his certifications, Eybrecht is a USTA High Performance Coach, a PTR Tennis Professional, a PTR Teaching Professional, a NSRSA Certified Stringer, and a NFHS Member. Eybrecht currently resides in Kirkland, Washington where he is currently focused on developing the first of many PNW Sports & Wellness Development Centers.